THE SPIRAL & THE FLAME

A GUIDED JOURNAL OF REMEMBRANCE & BECOMING

THE SPIRAL & THE FLAME

A Guided Journal of Remembrance & Becoming

Wisdom from the Guides Who Live Within

Copyright Page

First Edition: 2025

Published and distributed in Scottsdale, Arizona, USA:
Ink to Impact Publishing
Scottsdale, AZ 85255
Email: Natalie@InkToImpactPublishing.com

ISBN Hardcover: 978-1-968017-17-0
ISBN Print: 978-1-968017-16-3

Illustrations by: Kathleen Z. Carlson

Printed in the United States of America.

For information, bulk orders, or speaking engagements, please contact:
Kathleen@StraightUpSuccess.com

This is for the woman who gave everything
to hold it all together.
Who led, loved, and labored so hard that
somewhere along the way, she forgot herself.
This is your invitation to remember.
Not the version they praised.
Not the role you mastered.
But the you beneath it all.
The one who's been whispering,
"Come home."
This journal is a sacred mirror.
A place to reacquaint yourself...
With yourself.
Maybe for the first time.

Kathleen Carlson

Architect of Soul-Aligned Power.
Intuitive. Strategic. Unapologetically True.
I see what others miss and bring your life back into harmony, piece by sacred piece.

For the woman who's
been holding it all together.
For the one who whispers "maybe later"
to herself while showing up for everyone else.
For the seeker, the healer, the
high-achiever, the one
quietly unraveling and rising all at once.

This journal is for you.
May it become a refuge.
A reckoning.
A remembering.
And if no one told you lately;
You are holy ground.
You are not alone.

This is your time!

With reverence,

Kathleen

A whisper before the fire"

A BLESSING FOR YOUR BECOMING

You didn't find this journal by accident.
She's been calling to you.
She's been waiting for you to slow down long
enough to hear her whisper: It's time.
This isn't just paper and ink.
It's a mirror. A remembering.
A conversation with the part of you that's been
waiting to be seen.
Each word, each prompt, each breath you take
here is a doorway — guiding
you back to the woman you were always becoming.
You are not behind.
You are not broken.
You are not too late.
You are right on time for your own becoming.
This is where you drop the armor, release the noise,
and hear your own voice again,
the one that knows what's true, what's next, and
what's yours to claim.
Take a deep breath.
Step across the threshold.
The remembering begins now.

With love & fire,

Kathleen

MAY I INTRODUCE YOU TO YOUR GUIDED JOURNAL?

This isn't a journal you race through, it's one that walks beside you.
Within these pages, you'll find questions, reflections, and invitations
designed to meet you exactly where you are.

There's no wrong way to move through it.
You might begin at the first page,
or you might open to the one that calls to you.

Trust yourself, the right place is wherever you begin.
Some days, you'll write freely.
Other days, a single sentence or thought will be enough.
This space isn't asking for performance or perfection.
It's asking for your presence.

As you journey, you'll meet distinctive Guides,
each with their own element, energy, and wisdom.
They'll walk with you, helping you to remember who you are
beneath the shoulds, shame, and silence...
the noise of the world.
Let them surprise you. Let them speak.
You'll know when one of them has something to say.

These pages are both mirror and map,
reflecting what's true and guiding what's next.

Take your time.
Breathe.

Let the process unfold. You are not here to get it right.
You're here to come alive.

SETTING YOUR INTENTION

Before you begin, take a breath.

Let the noise fall away.

This moment is yours.
Place a hand over your heart and ask:
What do I most want to remember?
What part of me is ready to rise?
Don't overthink it.
Your intention doesn't need to sound poetic or perfect,
it only needs to feel true.
Let it be a phrase, a promise, or a prayer.
Let it be something that anchors you every time you return here.

Speak it out loud.

Whisper it if you must.

Write it below and let it live on the page as your quiet commitment to yourself.

This is where your journey begins.

Return to this page when you need to remember.

ELAVARI

The one who remembers when you forget.

Matriarch Elder – Earth Element
Bend like the willow, but never break.

Who She Is

Elavari is the embodiment of Earth wisdom, ancient resilience, and sacred lineage.
She holds the stories of your ancestors, the truths buried in your bones, and the knowing that you have already survived storms stronger than this.
She is the heartbeat beneath the chaos, the warm soil that softens your fall and the soft voice that whispers...
"Root deeper."
She comes to you when your foundation feels shaken, when you've forgotten the strength of your own becoming, or when life calls you to return home to yourself.

When to Call Her

Before beginning deep reflection, forgiveness, or letting go
When healing family patterns or ancestral wounds
When you feel ungrounded, scattered, or overwhelmed
During times of transition or emotional turbulence
When you need to feel safe, held, and unbreakable

Invocation

Place your hands on your heart or over the earth.
Breathe into your belly. Speak aloud:
"Elavari, Matriarch of Earth, Rootkeeper of all that is true guide me back to what is eternal.

Elavari reminds you: you do not have to hold it all alone."
She is not far. She lives in your breath. In your bones.
In the remembering.

Elavari-Aligned Journal Prompts

Each one a sacred invitation on the path home to self.

Rooted Remembering

What parts of me feels disconnected from my center?

"Bend like the willow, but never break."

Elavari-Aligned Journal Prompts

Each one a sacred invitation on the path home to self.

Where do I need to slow down
and ground myself?

"Bend like the willow, but never break."

Elavari-Aligned Journal Prompts

Each one a sacred invitation on the path home to self.

What has grief taught me about who I am?

"Bend like the willow, but never break."

Elavari-Aligned Journal Prompts

Each one a sacred invitation on the path home to self.

What ancestral strength lives in my bones?

"Bend like the willow, but never break."

Elavari-Aligned Journal Prompts

Each one a sacred invitation on the path home to self.

Where do I feel most at home in my body?

"Bend like the willow, but never break."

Elavari-Aligned Journal Prompts

Each one a sacred invitation on the path home to self.

What does it mean to me to be "deeply rooted"?

"Bend like the willow, but never break."

Elavari-Aligned Journal Prompts

Each one a sacred invitation on the path home to self.

When do I feel most like myself?

"Bend like the willow, but never break."

Elavari-Aligned Journal Prompts

Each one a sacred invitation on the path home to self.

Rooted Remembering

What stories or roles am I ready to lay down?

"Bend like the willow, but never break."

Elavari-Aligned Journal Prompts

Each one a sacred invitation on the path home to self.

Rooted Remembering

What is whispering beneath the noise?

"Bend like the willow, but never break."

Elavari-Aligned Journal Prompts

Each one a sacred invitation on the path home to self.

What does stillness offer me?

"Bend like the willow, but never break."

Elavari-Aligned Journal Prompts

Each one a sacred invitation on the path home to self.

How does nature reflect my own inner seasons?

"Bend like the willow, but never break."

Elavari-Aligned Journal Prompts

Each one a sacred invitation on the path home to self.

Earth as Mirror

What cycle am I in right now,
beginning, middle, or end?

"Bend like the willow, but never break."

Elavari-Aligned Journal Prompts

Each one a sacred invitation on the path home to self.

Earth as Mirror

What am I composting in my life?

"Bend like the willow, but never break."

Elavari-Aligned Journal Prompts

Each one a sacred invitation on the path home to self.

Earth as Mirror

What do I need to forgive myself for?

"Bend like the willow, but never break."

Elavari-Aligned Journal Prompts

Each one a sacred invitation on the path home to self.

Earth as Mirror

What are the rituals that keep me steady?

"Bend like the willow, but never break."

Elavari-Aligned Journal Prompts

Each one a sacred invitation on the path home to self.

Earth as Mirror

What kind of nourishment do I need, physically, emotionally, spiritually? ?

"Bend like the willow, but never break."

Elavari-Aligned Journal Prompts

Each one a sacred invitation on the path home to self.

Earth as Mirror

How do I respond when life asks me to pause?

"Bend like the willow, but never break."

Elavari-Aligned Journal Prompts

Each one a sacred invitation on the path home to self.

Earth as Mirror

What part of me is quietly growing?

"Bend like the willow, but never break."

Elavari-Aligned Journal Prompts

Each one a sacred invitation on the path home to self.

Earth as Mirror

Where am I resisting rest?

"Bend like the willow, but never break."

Elavari-Aligned Journal Prompts

Each one a sacred invitation on the path home to self.

What would it feel like to honor my slowness?

"Bend like the willow, but never break."

Elavari-Aligned Journal Prompts

Each one a sacred invitation on the path home to self.

What would my future elder self want me to know right now?

"Bend like the willow, but never break."

Elavari-Aligned Journal Prompts

Each one a sacred invitation on the path home to self.

What kind of wisdom do I already carry?

"Bend like the willow, but never break."

Elavari-Aligned Journal Prompts

Each one a sacred invitation on the path home to self.

What legacy do I want to root into the world?

"Bend like the willow, but never break."

Elavari-Aligned Journal Prompts

Each one a sacred invitation on the path home to self.

What truths have only revealed themselves in stillness?

"Bend like the willow, but never break."

Elavari-Aligned Journal Prompts

Each one a sacred invitation on the path home to self.

What rhythms does my soul crave?

"Bend like the willow, but never break."

Elavari-Aligned Journal Prompts

Each one a sacred invitation on the path home to self.

When have I let softness lead?

"Bend like the willow, but never break."

Elavari-Aligned Journal Prompts

Each one a sacred invitation on the path home to self.

What would it feel like to be deeply unshakable?

"Bend like the willow, but never break."

Elavari-Aligned Journal Prompts

Each one a sacred invitation on the path home to self.

What can I learn from the trees?

"Bend like the willow, but never break."

Elavari-Aligned Journal Prompts

Each one a sacred invitation on the path home to self.

What does it mean to embody grace?

"Bend like the willow, but never break."

Elavari-Aligned Journal Prompts

Each one a sacred invitation on the path home to self.

Earth as Mirror

What part of me is ready to take root?

"Bend like the willow, but never break."

KAELITH

The One Who Burns Away Illusion to Reveal the Truth

Warrior Guardian – Fire Element

NO ONE ENTERS YOUR FIELD WITHOUT HONOR

WHO SHE IS

Kaelith embodies sacred strength—your inner warrior wrapped in wisdom.
With a shield in one hand and purpose in the other,
she appears when you're tempted to shrink or stay silent.
She is the guardian of your inner fire—the force that protects, purifies,
and propels. She carries ancient codes of resilience, honor, and boundary.
Fierce yet faithful, Kaelith reminds you
True power is not aggression—but aligned protection.
Her flame is not for destruction. It is for revelation.

WHEN to CALL HER

When you feel timid, silenced, or like you're losing ground
When "being nice" is costing you your truth
When fear shows up dressed as people-pleasing
When you're ready to burn the mask and reveal your true power
When you're stepping into leadership, visibility, or bold expression

INVOCATION

Kaelith, fire-bearer of truth,
Stand with me in moments of fear.
Let your flame burn through what no longer serves.
Place your shield at my back
And your sword in my hand
So I may walk forward not in violence,
But in power.
Not in reaction,
But in remembrance.
I claim my sacred ground.
I remember my strength.
I rise.

Kaelith-Aligned Journal Prompts

Summons the Strength Within You.

Ignite The Inner Fire

What makes you feel powerful, not performative,
but truly alive in your skin?

"No one enters your field without honor."

Kaelith-Aligned Journal Prompts

Summons the Strength Within You.

Ignite The Inner Fire

Where in your life are you shrinking to stay safe?

"No one enters your field without honor."

Kaelith-Aligned Journal Prompts

Summons the Strength Within You.

When was the last time you felt truly brave?
What happened?

"No one enters your field without honor."

Kaelith-Aligned Journal Prompts

Summons the Strength Within You.

Ignite The Inner Fire

What is your relationship with anger and What might it be trying to protect?

"No one enters your field without honor."

Kaelith-Aligned Journal Prompts

Summons the Strength Within You.

Ignite The Inner Fire

How do you hold yourself accountable without self-punishment?

"No one enters your field without honor."

Kaelith-Aligned Journal Prompts

Summons the Strength Within You.

Ignite The Inner Fire

Who taught you what it means to be "strong"?
Do you still believe that?

"No one enters your field without honor."

Kaelith-Aligned Journal Prompts

Summons the Strength Within You.

Ignite The Inner Fire

When have you witnessed your own resilience?

"No one enters your field without honor."

Kaelith-Aligned Journal Prompts

Summons the Strength Within You.

What does your fire feel like when it's balanced vs. when it's overwhelming?

"No one enters your field without honor."

Kaelith-Aligned Journal Prompts

Summons the Strength Within You.

Ignite The Inner Fire

How do you protect your own energy right now and is it working?

"No one enters your field without honor."

Kaelith-Aligned Journal Prompts

Summons the Strength Within You.

Ignite The Inner Fire

What scares you about being truly powerful?

"No one enters your field without honor."

Kaelith-Aligned Journal Prompts

Summons the Strength Within You.

What boundaries need strengthening and which ones are ready to soften?

"No one enters your field without honor."

Kaelith-Aligned Journal Prompts

Summons the Strength Within You.

Where are you leaking your energy out of guilt, duty, or habit?

"No one enters your field without honor."

Kaelith-Aligned Journal Prompts

Summons the Strength Within You.

What truth have you been carrying silently, and why?

"No one enters your field without honor."

Kaelith-Aligned Journal Prompts

Summons the Strength Within You.

If you were to honor your time like it was sacred, what would shift?

"No one enters your field without honor."

Kaelith-Aligned Journal Prompts

Summons the Strength Within You.

What does energetic consent look like in your relationships?

"No one enters your field without honor."

Kaelith-Aligned Journal Prompts

Summons the Strength Within You.

What parts of your story no longer need defending?

"No one enters your field without honor."

Kaelith-Aligned Journal Prompts

Summons the Strength Within You.

Who or what drains your fire the most?

"No one enters your field without honor."

Kaelith-Aligned Journal Prompts

Summons the Strength Within You.

What does healthy confrontation mean to you?

"No one enters your field without honor."

Kaelith-Aligned Journal Prompts

Summons the Strength Within You.

What helps you recover after emotional battle or burn-out?

"No one enters your field without honor."

Kaelith-Aligned Journal Prompts

Summons the Strength Within You.

Where do you still confuse peace with people-pleasing?

"No one enters your field without honor."

Kaelith-Aligned Journal Prompts

Summons the Strength Within You.

Lead with Fire In Your Heart

What kind of leader are you becoming?

"No one enters your field without honor."

Kaelith-Aligned Journal Prompts

Summons the Strength Within You.

Lead with Fire In Your Heart

How do you honor your intuition while staying grounded in reality?

"No one enters your field without honor.'

Kaelith-Aligned Journal Prompts

Summons the Strength Within You.

Lead with Fire In Your Heart

What does it look like to protect without control?

"No one enters your field without honor."

Kaelith-Aligned Journal Prompts

Summons the Strength Within You.

Where in your life are you
called to show up more fiercely right now?

"No one enters your field without honor."

Kaelith-Aligned Journal Prompts

Summons the Strength Within You.

Lead with Fire In Your Heart

What core values are you unwilling to compromise on?

"No one enters your field without honor."

Kaelith-Aligned Journal Prompts

Summons the Strength Within You.

Lead with Fire In Your Heart

What would Kaelith say about the way you speak to yourself?

"No one enters your field without honor."

Kaelith-Aligned Journal Prompts

Summons the Strength Within You.

Lead with Fire In Your Heart

When do you feel most connected to your mission or life's purpose?

"No one enters your field without honor."

Kaelith-Aligned Journal Prompts

Summons the Strength Within You.

Lead with Fire In Your Heart

How do you want to use your fire in service, not just in survival?

"No one enters your field without honor."

Kaelith-Aligned Journal Prompts

Summons the Strength Within You.

Lead with Fire In Your Heart

What kind of legacy do you want to leave with your voice, your actions, your love?

"No one enters your field without honor."

Kaelith-Aligned Journal Prompts

Summons the Strength Within You.

Lead with Fire In Your Heart

Finish this sentence: "I lead with fire when..."

"No one enters your field without honor."

ORIELLE

The one in full celestial clarity, with her feet on the ground and her spirit in the stars.

Light Weaver – Ether Element

Bend like the willow, but never break

Who She Is

Orielle is the quiet breath before revelation,the hush between moonrise and sunrise.

She is the translator of soul whispers.

She brings the sudden knowing that wasn't taught but simply remembered.

She's part cosmic cartographer, part inner voice amplified.

She waits until you're still enough to hear the truth behind your thoughts.

Then she leans in, and says what you already knew, but were afraid to believe.

Her essence is air and stardust, clarity and curiosity.

When to Call Her

Call Orielle when your mind is noisy, your intuition muted.

When you're drifting but can't tell whether it's directionless or divine.

When you crave elevation—not escape.

When you're overthinking, under-trusting, and desperately need to feel the breeze of truth move through you again.

Orielle won't hand you the map. She'll help you become it.

INVOCATION

Orielle, star-sister and weaver of light,
Wrap me in the threads of the Infinite.
Remind me I am not lost—only remembering.
Lift the veil from my inner sight.
Let my voice echo truth from ancient stars,
And let silence speak in sacred code.
Through you, I return to the wisdom I carry.
Through you, I rise in resonance.

And, So it is.

Orielle-Aligned Journal Prompts

Remember The Truth You have Always Carried.

What is my inner voice trying to tell me right now?

"You already encoded this. I'm just here to remind you.

Where have I been looking for answers outside of myself?

"You already encoded this. I'm just here to remind you."

What is fogging up my clarity?

"You already encoded this. I'm just here to remind you."

Orielle-Aligned Journal Prompts

Remember The Truth You have Always Carried.

What thoughts or stories are no longer mine to carry?

"You already encoded this. I'm just here to remind you."

When do I feel most connected to my inner knowing?

"You already encoded this. I'm just here to remind you."

What does truth feel like in my body?

"You already encoded this. I'm just here to remind you."

Orielle-Aligned Journal Prompts

Remember The Truth You have Always Carried.

What am I being invited to release?

"You already encoded this. I'm just here to remind you."

Where is the resistance actually rooted in fear?

"You already encoded this. I'm just here to remind you.

Orielle-Aligned Journal Prompts

Remember The Truth You have Always Carried.

How does my soul communicate with me?

"You already encoded this. I'm just here to remind you."

Orielle-Aligned Journal Prompts

Remember The Truth You have Always Carried.

What sacred signal keeps showing up again and again?

"You already encoded this. I'm just here to remind you."

Orielle-Aligned Journal Prompts

Remember The Truth You have Always Carried.

What part of me is remembering something ancient?

"You already encoded this. I'm just here to remind you."

Orielle-Aligned Journal Prompts

Remember The Truth You have Always Carried.

When have I ignored my intuition and paid the price?

"You already encoded this. I'm just here to remind you."

Orielle-Aligned Journal Prompts

Remember The Truth You have Always Carried.

How can I become a better listener to my inner truth?

"You already encoded this. I'm just here to remind you."

What repeating pattern is calling me to pause and reflect?

"You already encoded this. I'm just here to remind you."

What cosmic lesson am I in right now?

"You already encoded this. I'm just here to remind you."

Orielle-Aligned Journal Prompts

Remember The Truth You have Always Carried.

What energies feel expansive vs. constrictive?

"You already encoded this. I'm just here to remind you."

Orielle-Aligned Journal Prompts

Remember The Truth You have Always Carried.

What beliefs did I outgrow but haven't released yet?

"You already encoded this. I'm just here to remind you."

Orielle-Aligned Journal Prompts

Remember The Truth You have Always Carried.

What does spaciousness feel like in my life?

"You already encoded this. I'm just here to remind you."

When am I most in flow?

"You already encoded this. I'm just here to remind you."

What messages have come to me in dreams, symbols, or synchronicities?

"You already encoded this. I'm just here to remind you."

Orielle-Aligned Journal Prompts

Remember The Truth You have Always Carried.

What does soul-aligned success look like to me?

"You already encoded this. I'm just here to remind you."

Orielle-Aligned Journal Prompts

Remember The Truth You have Always Carried.

How do I want to feel in my future?

"You already encoded this. I'm just here to remind you."

Orielle-Aligned Journal Prompts

Remember The Truth You have Always Carried.

What would I do if I trusted myself completely?

"You already encoded this. I'm just here to remind you."

Orielle-Aligned Journal Prompts

Remember The Truth You have Always Carried.

What ideas are whispering for me to follow?

"You already encoded this. I'm just here to remind you."

Orielle-Aligned Journal Prompts

Remember The Truth You have Always Carried.

What timeline am I ready to leave behind?

"You already encoded this. I'm just here to remind you."

Orielle-Aligned Journal Prompts

Remember The Truth You have Always Carried.

How can I align with my highest self today?

"You already encoded this. I'm just here to remind you."

Orielle-Aligned Journal Prompts

Remember The Truth You have Always Carried.

What would Orielle say
if she could speak to me right now?

"You already encoded this. I'm just here to remind you."

Orielle-Aligned Journal Prompts

Remember The Truth You have Always Carried.

What truth have I always known but forgotten?

"You already encoded this. I'm just here to remind you."

Orielle-Aligned Journal Prompts

Remember The Truth You have Always Carried.

Where is my future calling me forward?

"You already encoded this. I'm just here to remind you."

Orielle-Aligned Journal Prompts

Remember The Truth You have Always Carried.

What am I ready to claim, embody, and remember?

"You already encoded this. I'm just here to remind you."

YOURSELF

The Guide of Becoming, Embodiment, and Divine Timeline Alignment

Beacon of Becoming – Light Element

"You are already her. She's just waiting for you to catch up."

Who She Is

A mirror of your wholeness. A reflection of your becoming.
She is not ahead of you. She is within you.
This is not about striving, fixing, or earning your worth.
It is the sacred returning.The gentle unfolding.
The knowing that you are not becoming someone new
you are remembering someone ancient, radiant, and already whole.
She is the version of you who moves from embodied truth.
The one who has alchemized the ache into wisdom, the fear into fire.
She speaks in symbols, light, and silence.
She knows your name.She sees your soul.
Now is the moment to rise into her frequency,
to meet her gaze with reverence and readiness,
to become the one you were always meant to be.

When to Call Her

Call on her when you feel stuck in the past or spinning in the now.
She appears when you're making decisions from fear,
when you forget how far you've come,
and when you need to borrow the calm of who you're becoming.

Invocation

I call upon my Future Self, beacon of clarity and becoming.
Show me the choices that bring me closer.
Help me listen with vision, move with purpose,
and remember my encoded wisdom.

Yourself-Aligned Journal Prompts

She's right behind your next brave choice.

Who is the woman I'm becoming?

"You are already her. She's just waiting for you to catch up."

Yourself-Aligned Journal Prompts

She's right behind your next brave choice.

What do I admire in her that's already mine?

"You are already her. She's just waiting for you to catch up."

Yourself-Aligned Journal Prompts

She's right behind your next brave choice.

Where in my life am I already embodying her?

"You are already her. She's just waiting for you to catch up."

Yourself-Aligned Journal Prompts

She's right behind your next brave choice.

What qualities does she live by?

"You are already her. She's just waiting for you to catch up."

Yourself-Aligned Journal Prompts

She's right behind your next brave choice.

What am I still afraid to claim?

"You are already her. She's just waiting for you to catch up."

How would she speak to me today?

"You are already her. She's just waiting for you to catch up."

What does it mean to "be her now"

"You are already her. She's just waiting for you to catch up."

She's right behind your next brave choice.

Where have I grown beyond my past identity?

"You are already her. She's just waiting for you to catch up."

Yourself-Aligned Journal Prompts

She's right behind your next brave choice.

What's one habit she has that I can try today?

"You are already her. She's just waiting for you to catch up."

She's right behind your next brave choice.

How would she spend her time?

"You are already her. She's just waiting for you to catch up."

Yourself-Aligned Journal Prompts

She's right behind your next brave choice.

What old stories need releasing to become her?

"You are already her. She's just waiting for you to catch up."

What version of me am I outgrowing?

"You are already her. She's just waiting for you to catch up."

What are the core beliefs of my Future Self?

"You are already her. She's just waiting for you to catch up."

Yourself-Aligned Journal Prompts

She's right behind your next brave choice.

What does she no longer tolerate?

"You are already her. She's just waiting for you to catch up."

What would it feel like to walk into a room as her?

"You are already her. She's just waiting for you to catch up."

What relationships or boundaries does she hold?

"You are already her. She's just waiting for you to catch up."

How does she make aligned decisions?

"You are already her. She's just waiting for you to catch up."

What rituals or practices does she honor?

"You are already her. She's just waiting for you to catch up."

Yourself-Aligned Journal Prompts

She's right behind your next brave choice.

What does she create effortlessly?

"You are already her. She's just waiting for you to catch up."

What kind of woman surrounds her?

"You are already her. She's just waiting for you to catch up."

Yourself-Aligned Journal Prompts

She's right behind your next brave choice.

What am I postponing that she would move on today?

"You are already her. She's just waiting for you to catch up."

Yourself-Aligned Journal Prompts

She's right behind your next brave choice.

What message is she sending me now?

"You are already her. She's just waiting for you to catch up."

Yourself-Aligned Journal Prompts

She's right behind your next brave choice.

What is one fear I am ready to alchemize?

"You are already her. She's just waiting for you to catch up."

Yourself-Aligned Journal Prompts

She's right behind your next brave choice.

What does presence feel like to her?

"You are already her. She's just waiting for you to catch up."

Yourself-Aligned Journal Prompts

She's right behind your next brave choice.

How does she self-regulate or return to calm?

"You are already her. She's just waiting for you to catch up."

Yourself-Aligned Journal Prompts

She's right behind your next brave choice.

What does her energy feel like, physically, emotionally, spiritually?

"You are already her. She's just waiting for you to catch up."

Yourself-Aligned Journal Prompts

She's right behind your next brave choice.

What is she celebrating me for already?

"You are already her. She's just waiting for you to catch up."

Yourself-Aligned Journal Prompts

She's right behind your next brave choice.

What kind of impact does she have on others?

"You are already her. She's just waiting for you to catch up."

Yourself-Aligned Journal Prompts

She's right behind your next brave choice.

What is her legacy?

"You are already her. She's just waiting for you to catch up."

Yourself-Aligned Journal Prompts

She's right behind your next brave choice.

What would change if I stopped waiting and started living as her today?

"You are already her. She's just waiting for you to catch up."

The Journey Isn't Over

Dear Fellow Journeyer,

If you've made it to this page, something in these spirals and flames lit a spark in you. I want you to know, you're not alone. Whether you've scribbled in the margins or poured your heart into every prompt, your presence here means something. You've said yes to remembering. You've said yes to becoming.

This isn't the end. It's a breath. A pause before the next rise. You can keep exploring, keep becoming, and keep walking this sacred path at your own pace, in your own rhythm. And if you're ready to continue this work alongside others who are remembering too, there's a place for you.

You're invited to join us inside The Remembering Room... a cozy, radiant corner of the internet where soul-led women gather to reflect, rise, and whatever comes next. You'll find support, inspiration, and maybe even the reminder you didn't know you were searching for.

And if you're curious what else is unfolding, StraightUpSuccess.com is the place to land. That's where you'll find my work, my latest musings, and... even more ways to walk this journey together.

Let this be the beginning of something holy, fierce, and completely yours.

Because yes, you can have it all...
once you figure out what "it" really is.

With love and fire,
Kathleen

Come join us here:
www.StraightUpSuccess.com
Facebook group: The Remembering Room
A Spiral & Flame Community
Or scan the QR code to step in now.

About the Author

Kathleen Carlson is a truth-teller, intuitive guide, and executive mentor for women ready to stop performing and start becoming.

After decades leading multi-million-dollar teams in the corporate world, she now leads a movement of soul-led female leaders ready to reclaim their wholeness, rewrite their stories, and rise on their own terms.

Through her signature journal The Spiral & The Flame, her "Straight Up Success" philosophy, and her embodied leadership work, Kathleen helps women remember who they are beneath the noise, powerful, wise, and wildly capable.

Her work lives at the intersection of strategy and soul, grounding big vision in real-world impact.

Follow Kathleen:

https://www.straightupsuccess.com
https://www.linkedin.com/in/kathleen-carlson-a05779a8/

Made in the USA
Las Vegas, NV
11 November 2025

45e48375-c82a-4829-bb80-1469fc8135ecR01